STARK |

A FAMILY IN FEAR

A STORY OF DOMESTIC VIOLENCE

PENNY EVERHART

PAGE PUBLISHING, INC.
Conneaut Lake, PA

First originally published by Page Publishing 2020

Some names have been changed to protect the privacy of individuals

ISBN 978-1-64544-542-5 (pbk)
ISBN 978-1-6624-0391-0 (hc)
ISBN 978-1-64544-543-2 (digital)

Printed in the United States of America

In loving memory of my beloved sister,
wish you could be here to share this with me,
and to all the men and women who have
died at the hands of domestic violence,
rest in peace, Godspeed.
And to all survivors, the inspiration to others.

FOREWORD

There are two types of people in the world: cowards and the courageous.

Cowards—we all know them, can name them, can see them in our past, across the rooms and in our lives. Some cower, timid, with darting eyes, bowed head, hood or collar or scarf too high about their face. Afraid of taking their place in the world, a stand on an issue or sometimes just the next step, these are people to whom fear is self-paralyzing. Their cowardice limits them, and it saddens that they suffer in that way.

There are other cowards, though, whom engender no pity, no empathy, no sorrow. Those that hide their fear behind bullying and intimidation and violence, who use physical power to hide mental pain, who transfer their own hurt by hurting others—those people are, simply put, monsters—chickenshit monsters, to be sure, but monsters, nonetheless. To inflict lasting wounds or try to because they themselves are wounded? Gutless and shameful.

And then there are the courageous—brave, resilient, tough-as-nails humans who fight through all measure of adversity (and Lord knows we all face it); people who get that life is a test, one they refuse to fail—who get up when knocked down, who stand up for what's right, who treat others with kindness and respect, who love big and risk much and, in the end, live lives that make positive difference in the world.

Two types of people: cowards and the courageous. Penny Everhart's courage is remarkable, and her story is vitally important to read and reflect upon. We are blessed that she took the time to share it, if by doing so, she saves even one other from the assault and abuse that marked so much of her life—well, then, she is, in fact, a hero of the highest regard.

—Joseph Seivold

ACKNOWLEDGMENTS

I want to express my love and appreciation to my mother and father for all the support and love you have given myself and your grandchildren, you have gone above what you do for your family, and I truly appreciate it.

To my brother and sister-in-law, Tim and Donna, thank you for the financial support when we needed it. You didn't know how bad it was but helped anyway. You will never know how much your love and support means to me.

To Mima and Abella, you are the kindest people I have ever met. Thank you for bringing me in your family and treating me like your daughter, and still do I will always love you and will be here if you ever need me.

To my best friends from school, Mary and Henry, I have known you forever. My other sister and brother, you have been with me through good and bad, supported me emotionally. I am so blessed to have you in my life. I love you.

And to all my friends, you make me feel loved. I love you all.

A special thank-you to Joseph Sievold for writing the foreword. I appreciate the kindness you have shown me since I started working for you. Thank you so much for taking the time out of your busy schedule of running Berkeley Preparatory School. I greatly appreciate it.

And last, my children, who I love more than anything. I wish I could have made your life easier, but I will try to make it up to you. I love you more than you know.

And a very special thank you to Peggy, my sister from another mother. I might not be here if not for you when he came to work trying to see me at four in the morning. You handled him by not letting him in and being strong with him when I couldn't. Love you.

My Heroes

PENNY EVERHART

INTRODUCTION

I had kept a lot of secret things no one knew but me and him; my kids didn't even know a lot of what happened.

But I decided to write this book for two reasons: first to help other men and women understand why it's not that easy to leave an abusive relationship. It's easy to say just leave, but not everyone is that strong.

The second reason is to rid myself of all the old feelings and to hopefully move on without some of the sadness, and finally, let it all out.

I was worried how people would see me—I am very vulnerable. People who don't know me will have an impression of me by just reading this book, but if this helps, just one person leave an abusive relationship or just one person has that uncomfortable talk with someone they know that is being abused, it was worth it. So as I say in the book, "Take a walk in my shoes."

When I started telling people I wrote this book, I started hearing so many stories of people who were also abused, some had only told a few people. Hopefully, that's what this book will do: open up conversations about this epidemic conversations with parents to their children so they are aware of the signs because it can start at the dating stage, which is where it should also end hopefully.

For my friends and
Family who were always
There for me, my father
For giving me hugs when
I needed them, and I
Needed a lot writing this book
And for my children, I love you

As I was sitting in the domestic violence
Class for the victims of abuse, I thought to
Myself, *How did I get here*? I was sitting
With around ten to fifteen women who were there
For the same reason—their husbands, boyfriends
Or significant other had beat them.
They were all different black, white, Hispanic,
Young, old, poor, and well-to-do.
Abuse I come to find out does not discriminate,
Oh yes, I was one of those women who
Thought why does any person stay in
An abusive relationship, why don't they just
Leave.
Well, now, being one of those abused women,
I can tell you from experience…it's not
That easy.
There is a saying, "Don't judge someone until
You've walked a mile in their shoes."
To walk in my shoes, keep reading…

Small steps in the right direction can turn
out to be the biggest step of your life.
—Unknown

My story is by no means unique; abuse happens every day. Some women like me are the lucky ones, the ones who live to tell their story. Some are not so fortunate for men who abuse them often end up killing them then themselves. I never thought I would be a statistic, but I am one out of ten million Americans who are victims of physical violence annually according to the National Coalition Against Domestic Violence. Forty to forty-five is the percentage of women physically abused who are raped and or assaulted during the relationship.

A woman is beaten every nine seconds in the US. Eighty-one percent of women who are stalked by a current or former male partner who are also physically abused by their partner. Women who are victims of domestic violence are eight times more likely to be killed by an intimate partner if there are firearms in the house. And 98 percent of financial abuse occurs in all domestic violence cases. This is the number one reason domestic violence survivors stay or return to abusive relationships—the abuser controls their money supply.

Twenty people are victims of physical violence every minute in the United States and one in three women and one and four men is a victim of some form of physical violence.

Domestic Violence accounts for fourteen percent of all violent crime in the United States.

These are just a few statistics I will be giving you throughout the book. You, like me, probably didn't realize how high the figures were. It was a real eye opener.

I can't change the direction of the wind, but I can adjust my sails to always reach my destination.

—Jimmy Dean

EFFECTS OF
DOMESTIC VIOLENCE
ON CHILDREN

According to the US Department of Health and Human Resources, more than fifteen million children in the United States live in a house with domestic violence that has occurred at least once. They say a boy who has seen his mother abused are ten times more likely to abuse his female partner.

Also a girl who has grown up in a house where a father has abused her mother is more than six times as likely to be sexually abused as a girl who grows up in a non-abusive home.

The important thing to realize is children who witness or are victims of emotional, physical, sexual abuse are higher risk for health problems as adults.

Some includes...Mental and health conditions such as heart disease, diabetes, obesity and poor self-esteem.

I tell you this because my children have problems because of the abuse. My son, Matthew, was diagnosed with bipolar, low self-esteem, doesn't care if he lives.

Wade doesn't like confrontation, trusting men for my daughters is ongoing. These are just some statistics now you can see why people stay, it's not just easy to leave like I said until you walk in my shoes or anyone else's...

Nothing is impossible the word itself says "I'm possible!
—Audrey Hepburn

CHAPTER 1

The Exes

The Dog and the Thief

To say I have had bad luck with men would be an understatement. I have been married two times and both were disastrous. The first time was to Alex; he was from Cuba. We met in ninth grade. I guess you could say we were high school sweethearts. Alex was my first real love. We were married right out of high school; that was my first mistake.

I come to find out after we were married that Alex was still very immature. I wanted a family and kids, he wanted to race cars and be young and carefree. After five years of marriage, I became pregnant with our first and only child. What I thought would be the happiest time in my life became one of the worst. While I was eight months pregnant, I found out Alex was cheating on me with a girl from his work, who lived two streets from us. To let you know what kind of girl we're talking about, she came in my house while I was working and had sex with my husband in my bed. She knew he was married and that I was pregnant, but that didn't stop either one of them.

I'm not saying I am a saint or perfect, but no one deserves that. He never tried to talk to me about our marriage or try to save it.

Try to be a rainbow in someone else's cloud.
—Maya Angelou

The reason I told you—he was Cuban and by the way, she was Hispanic—also is to let you know dogs come in all colors, shapes, and sizes.

I know you're wondering if they're still together. The answer is yes. We got divorced after our daughter was born, and a few years later, they got married and had kids, but you have to think there are trust issues in that relationship because they are both cheaters and have low moral values.

But I digress, yes, I know I sound a little bitter, just a little who am I kidding. I'm a lot bitter; they had sex in my bed in my house while I was eight months pregnant. Do you blame me?

Enough about him on to marriage number two.

After the divorce, I got custody of my beautiful daughter, Chloe. He received visitation. Alex had to pay child support payments I was working as a manager in a store my parents built a room on so Chloe and I could move in with them, and they would watch Chloe while I worked. Chloe was the first grandchild on both sides, and just let me say, Alex's parents are the nicest people. They treated me like a daughter they never had. Alex had two other brothers, no sisters; they could not help how their son was.

Anyway, I met Alan at a bar, which in itself should have been a red flag, but you have to understand I am not the type to smoke, drink, or even use bad language. Pretty much a square, but all I did was work and take care of Chloe and on that one.

Saturday night, my cousins and a family friend wanted to get me out. My daughter was three months old, and I just needed a night out after the previous months. I was mentally drained. Anyway, he was there; we met exchanged numbers and a couple of weeks went by, and I didn't hear anything from him, thought nothing about it, went about my business working, taking care of Chloe.

Around three weeks later he called, we started dating, and let me tell you, they say opposites attract. We were opposite in every way. He smoked, I didn't. He drank, I didn't. He used bad language, I didn't, but what can I say, you can't help who you fall in love with. He was handsome and nice, and I think it just felt good to have someone, love me again I missed that feeling after everything I had been through. Thinking back now, I should have taken more time for myself and work through my feelings, but God does things for a reason. He told me his mom died a year before, and he was the youngest of five—two sisters and two other brothers. He also told me his father abused his mother and that his father was an alcoholic that had left them when he was little, his father who I never met, passed away while we were married.

I tell you this just to give you a little background on him and why he was like he was also abuse is a cycle. Alan and his siblings have addictive personalities. My children do too. It's how you deal with it that make a difference. I always tell them you have to be careful in everything you do, everything in moderation, it would be so easy for any vice to turn into something more. Alan's family have all had some form of addiction. Anyway, six months later we were living together and within a year married. On our wedding day, I got a glimpse of things to come…

We had the wedding and reception at Alan's sister's house; it was beautiful. The sun was setting, could not have asked for a more beautiful day.

After the wedding, the party started around an hour. Into it, I couldn't find Alan. When I finally did find him, he said four of his friends had gotten some cocaine for him, a wedding present, and they had gone somewhere to do it. Now you're probably thinking, did he do this before? Well, not that I know of. I was just as shocked as you are reading about it.

Yes, I know he smoked pot but not around my daughter. Also at the time, he had a good job, was working their, was nothing to make me think he was doing anything stronger than marijuana. He told me it was just for today he wouldn't do it again. And like I said, he was nice, but that would change.

We were married for twenty-eight years. I know you will read this chapter after chapter and think when is she leaving this jerk, but as you read, you will see it wasn't easy.

It's never too late to be what you might have been.
—George Eliot

Abuse they say is never a onetime event, and that is so true, in my case, it was almost an everyday event toward the end.

If you don't know about abuse, which I didn't until it happened to me, *abuse* is "about power and control. Abusers will use intimidation, make you feel afraid by using looks, actions, gestures, smashing things and destroy your property, and if they have weapons will threaten you with them.

They will threaten you by saying they will kill you then commit suicide, threaten to report you to your company's Human Resource department or Department of Children and Families make you drop charges. They will make you ask for money, take your money, prevent you from keeping a job, this is called economic abuse.

They minimize, deny, and blame, making light of the abuse, not taking your concerns about it seriously,

Say the abuse didn't happen, shift the abuse say you caused it, and the big one, isolation, this is a big one. They control what you do, who you see and. Who you talk to they use jealousy to justify their actions.

Unlike the physical abuse the emotional abuse can be worse the scars from physical abuse can go away but the emotional abuse take a lot longer to heal if they ever do. With the emotional abuse he will put you down, make you feel bad about yourself, call you names, make you feel like you're crazy by playing mind games, they will humiliate you and make you feel guilty.

I found out all this from a class I had to take thanks to Alan more about that later, but he did all these things to me.

Alan did all of this to me he was a classic abuser, most abusers do the same thing that is they have the same characteristics. Some are worse than others, but they are more or less the same.

If you can relate to any of these, please get help. Go to someone you can trust—a friend or a family member. Don't hide anymore; someone will help.

CHAPTER 2

Early Years

Within the first five years, a few things happened. First, I had my son, Wade, nine months after we were married. So our family consisted of Chloe from my first marriage and Wade—a boy and girl. The years after should have been happy, but soon after Wade was born the abuse started.

Alan was working; I stayed home to raise the kids for a few years.

After Wade was born, Alan started drinking more, that's when the abuse started. At first I was shocked. I don't even remember why he hit me, but after he said he was sorry and it would never happen again, blah, blah, blah. I heard that a lot after that I know you're thinking why didn't she leave then well, he said he was sorry. I know, but I was naive at the time. No one had ever hit me like that. I thought he really meant it when he said he wouldn't do it again. I blocked out a lot, only in writing this book am I forced to remember. Remember he chipped my tooth, that's how I remember that it was the first time. Anyway, as the drinking got worse, he started staying out late going with friends and leaving me home with the kids. He started acting different, he was more quick to anger, he started getting possessive and jealous. I would go to the grocery store, and he would call me fifty times "What are you doing? Who are you with?" I had to rush and be home quickly, or I really got it.

Only I can change my life, No one can do it for me.

—Carol Burnett

It was around this time I thought it couldn't be just drinking he had to be doing, drugs also.

We were living in an apartment, and thank God my daughter, Chloe, was spending the night at my parents when someone knocked on the door and asked for Alan. He went to the door. The guy, he apparently knew asked if he could go to the bathroom. When he came out, he said something to Allan and then started hitting him. They started fighting. They went outside; I went to the door and said I had called the police and he left. I found out he owed him money for drugs. He would often get calls and hang up on them. Things like this happened throughout our marriage.

I know what you're thinking why haven't I left him yet, but by this time, I had two kids and hadn't gone back to work yet but keep reading. Alan had a good job for five years. Those were probably the only good years because at least, he was working. We did have some good times but not that many. In 1998, he got arrested for domestic violence. He hit me. I called the police; he got out on his own recognize. He apologized, promised he would never do it again blah, blah, blah. By this time, he was wearing me down. I called him a thief at the beginning because he took my self-esteem, my strength who I was away, a little at a time, a beating at a time. I started to lose who I was; I didn't even recognize myself.

Eight years after Wade was born, we had Matt, my middle son. He was born on my birthday, and it happened to be Easter that year while I was pregnant.

With Matt, Al got arrested for trying to pick up a prostitute, who happened to be an undercover cop. Well, when he told me I was humiliated, he told me he just wanted to find out how much they charged. He was curious really, wow, how stupid did he think I was, but once again, I'm sorry I wasn't really wanting to get a prostitute blah, blah, blah. At that point, I thought what else could happen, well, a lot, just keep reading. The favorite thing he liked to do when he started hitting me was pulling my fingers back. I remember I had started back at work, and he had bent my thumb back so hard it was sprained, but I went to work, and it was painful, but no one knew. I was getting really good at hiding it.

To this day, one of my fingers is crocked from him pulling my fingers back. Sometimes, well, most of the time, I would go to bed only to be awaken by him, ranting and raving about how I'm cheating on him, needless to say, I got little sleep. A lot of times I would end up crying myself to sleep.

A diamond is a chunk of coal that did well under pressure.
—Unknown

CHAPTER 3

So Much Abuse

In this book are just some instances of abuse, but there was so much in the twenty-eight years to put in, a lot is repetition, and anyone who has been in an abusive relationship will tell you it is the same thing over and over. It is called a cycle, for a reason, it is about power.

Not to say there wasn't good times in between the beatings, there is the honeymoon phases. I am sorry it will never happen again. I love you, please don't leave me.

You want to believe them, but at that point, you are so beaten down. Any love he gives you is welcomed, but it never lasts. Then the nightmare starts over and over again.

At times, I would go to my parents to visit. My mom would see a bruise I couldn't hide, and believe me, I got good at hiding them when she asked me about the bruise, I would say I hit it on something at work. Believe me, there were many times I wanted to say something, yell, it help me please, but I couldn't. I was so embarrassed and humiliated not even just that I was mad—mad at myself for letting it go on.

I am the kind of person that keeps everything inside and having this done to me made me keep every emotion I had inside.

I got to where I would make excuses for the way he would act.

But I had not yet had enough.

An abuser robs you of a lot of happy events.

At Christmas, I would be the one who got everything ready in the morning. He would sleep while I tried to make things as good and normal for the kids under the circumstances. I would try to compensate for what was going on.

I remember on Wade's first birthday. We were going to have a big party at the park. I had the food, cake, called everyone, but then he came home the day of the party after staying out all night and slept all day. I had to call everyone and cancel saying he was sick I was once again embarrassed thank God Wade wasn't old enough to know what happened. That's just one instance; there is many more.

I know you're thinking now if I was ready to leave not yet I'm a glutton for punishment as the abuse got worse, he would now spit in my face, call me names, bitch, whore, and the worst, the C-word if you're a woman. You know that is the worst to me. Anyway, one day, he was sleeping. I snuck out of bed and went to the bank to open an account of my own without him knowing it. I got to the bank, opened the account. I was telling the lady thank you when he walked in and started making a scene. I walked out as fast I could him right beside me. I got in the car; he was screaming, he hit the windshield then me, but it was worth it, I got my account.

I did all the things they tell you to do in the domestic violence class hide money, make an extra set of keys, hide your purse, but he would always find them.

He would keep me up all night, beating me, chocking me, but I would go to work because we needed the money. Every month, the electric would get shut off or the cable. I vowed I would never let it happen again when I get out of this nightmare.

You can't go back and change the beginning but you can start where you are and change the ending.
—CS. Lewis

CHAPTER 4

Things He Took from Me

Al took a lot from me the good times I should have had like when my granddaughter was born. I went to the hospital. Of course, he stayed at home. He never came up to the hospital to even see the baby. While I was waiting for the baby to arrive, he called me at least fifty times, "Who are you with? Where are you?" The same old thing he would do this at all events. When Chloe got married, he wasn't there.

I came to realize he wouldn't go to events with me because if he was with me, he couldn't accuse me of cheating on him, he would even make up things. He would say he saw me with someone and swear it happened.

He was never there when the kids got hurt. My son hurt his leg, had to get steel rods in his leg when he was sixteen. I went to the hospital with him. I was going to stay all night, but of course, he called and wanted me to go home. I told Wade I would be back first thing in the morning that he would sleep because they gave him something for pain. Over the years going to family events like Thanksgiving, Christmas, or just a family get together became nonexistent. I would make excuses why we couldn't go. It seemed like holidays were the worst for Alan; he would be more abusive so it just wasn't worth it to try to go and hide the bruises.

Needless to say, it became very lonely times the more the abuse happened. I tried to do everything right so I wouldn't set him off, but I quickly found out it didn't matter what I did. Things could be perfect, and he would still accuse me of cheating on him with anyone and everyone.

He called my boss at work and accused him of having an affair when he told me. I was so embarrassed. He said he called the police to tell them he threatened him so it was on record. A week later, he transferred to another store. Another time, he called my son's friend and accused him because he worked at the pizza place. We got pizza. I know poor Wade was embarrassed. Alan became really paranoid; he actually got a tape recorder and placed it where I couldn't see it, trying to tape me cheating on him. Needless to say, you could hear me watching TV and talking to the kids, but he swore the people on TV was a guy and me.

I would tell him I would not cheat on him, I would just leave him. I would not wish that on my worst enemy because it was done to me.

There is divorce, you don't have to cheat, but that didn't stop the abuse. One night, the kids had a couple of friends over to spend the night. He came in and had been doing drugs. He started ranting and raving. He locked the doors, got us in the family room, and wouldn't let us leave. He hit me in the head after hours, keeping us there. He took me to the bedroom and raped me for the first time. I was crying and trying to talk to him, but he wouldn't listen. I was so scared the kids would come in because he didn't lock the door. Finally it was over. He went to sleep; we all ran across the street at our friend's and called the police. He was arrested; that was his third offense. He was sentenced to fifteen months in prison.

That was the hardest fifteen months of my life. I was scared. My kids were young. Chloe was only sixteen, Wade was fourteen, Matt was only five, and Elaina was almost two.

I got a full-time job. Chloe had quit school and was watching Elaina till she turned two so I could put her in preschool. My poor Chloe had to grow up so fast. I felt so bad for her.

To say this was a hard time, would be an understatement.

The best time for new beginnings is now.
—Unknown

CHAPTER 5

Neighbors from Hell

Once upon a time, there were two brothers—oh, wait a minute—that sounds like a fairytale, but it was far from it, more like a nightmare. There were two brothers who lived across the street from us. My parents had been friends with theirs.

After we brought the house from my mother when my father passed away, the nightmare started—I should say got worse.

At first, Alan got along with them, but after time and the more drugs and drinking he did things, got worse.

When Alan went to prison for fifteen months, my life was falling apart. The stress was sometimes unbearable.

My youngest Elaina was only a year and a half, and Matthew was five. He was the hardest hit when he left, just imagine one moment your father is there, the next he's gone.

He started doing strange things at school and home. I took him to the pediatrician, and he diagnosed him with borderline bipolar. My life was a mess like I said, I had to get a full-time job. My sixteen year old Chloe was watching my one and a half year old, and my five year old was bipolar. I had no money. I was feeling hopeless, but I had to keep going.

But about the neighbors, the two brothers were living in their mother's house when she passed away. One was just waiting for the other to die so they could have the house to themselves. That's how cold they were put it this way. The father gave the mother a choice, me or the kids, they still live at home. They never left the mother, choose the kids so needless to say, father left.

Anyway, Alan and the brothers had started a feud, which lasted a long time.

I got into it with them because when Alan went to prison, if Matthew went outside, they would say things to him like "Your father is a jailbird or drug addict." This was a five-year-old. You can say what you want to me, but you better leave my kids alone.

Anyway, they would call code enforcement weekly on us for any little thing. When Alan went to prison, they called the Department of Children and Families on me. The police were called out and checked the house, making sure they had rooms, beds, and clean clothes. I couldn't believe it they asked if I needed food. I said no. The report was closed. I felt like a failure.

Nothing can dim the light that shines from within.
—Maya Angelou

CHAPTER 6

More of the Same

As the abuse escalated and the drugs took more of a hold on him, I found out he was on crack. It wasn't just me. He hit the walls, took a beating also, anything I loved or valued collections I had would get broken.

When he was beating me, he would rip my panties and bras. When I would have to buy new ones, he would say "who are you buying those for." The chocking started, I tried to keep what was going on as quiet as I could so the kids wouldn't hear, but that got harder to do the older they got.

Every day was like groundhogs day—the same thing over and over and over except the beatings were getting worse.

In 2000, I was pregnant with Elaina, three months to be exact when he beat me. I thought I would get a break from beatings while I was pregnant, but like before, it made no difference. The kids went to our friend's across the street, and the police was called. They took pictures of the bruises and took Alan to jail. I remember the officer saying as he left, "If you don't leave him, he will keep doing it." Those words haunted me. He was charged with aggravated battery on a female with ten-thousand-dollar bail.

He stayed in jail till he went to court, yes he got out and came home, I know what you're thinking why didn't she leave this jerk, but I was pregnant with three kids to take care of.

That wasn't the last time he was arrested. In between jail he would have to take anger management classes and got put on house arrest many times, which he could never do. He always broke it by either not paying his probation or doing something he wasn't supposed to.

The abuse got worse. He wasn't working steady from 2001 to 2012. I was the only one working a steady job. Thank God we got income tax back.

Remember I told you that there are periods of the honeymoon phase, not every day or week was bad. He would have times of regret or go to classes and be fine for a while, but it would never last.

Another statistic is that the United Nations development fund for women estimates that at least one of every three women globally, will be beaten, raped, or abused, during her lifetime. In most cases, the abuser is a member of her own family.

Difficult roads often lead to beautiful destinations.
—Unknown

CHAPTER 7

Shame

This is probably one of the hardest things for me to write.

One of the times, he raped me. I got pregnant, and one of the hardest decisions I had to make was get an abortion; it was not an easy decision or one I took lightly. I love children, but I was not going to bring another child in this relationship. It was not fair to the child and hard enough on the kids that were here. I think about that often. I pray to God that he forgives me and wrestle with myself about it, but I know at the time, it was for the best.

Alan was not happy about the abortion. He actually came to the place I was having it done to try to talk me out of it. My mom had taken me, and he showed up. I had it done, anyway, he would throw it in my face a lot. He knew it hurt me needless to say, I carry a lot of shame.

Shame for letting it go on.

Shame for what it did to my kids, took their innocence.

Shame for what it did to me.

But I still not had enough.

One Help Guide.org if you are being abused, remember you are not to blame for being battered or mistreated.

—You are not the cause of your partner's abusive behavior.

—You deserve to be treated with respect.

—You deserve a safe and happy life.

—And you are not alone. There are people who want to help you.

When Alan got out of jail, we went back to our normal when one night he started my daughter. Elaina was going to call the police; he slapped the phone out of her hands. The police came arrested him, and he was convicted of hindering the report of a crime tampering with a witness.

This is when the end is finally near, but I also had to go to domestic violence classes, which takes us back to where the book begins. I had to take them because I let it go on, and the kids had seen it that night. My son had come between myself and Alan so he had got a mark above his eye. The police called the Department of Children and Families and they interviewed the kids and me separately. They told me they would take my kids away from me for letting it go on if I did not take the classes. He also had to take classes. They treated me like I was the worst mother in the world. Believe me, I didn't need them to tell me that the kids didn't need to be around this, but they treated me like I was a child abuser that hit my children.

For the next six months, they came to my house, took pictures of my children and their rooms; it was embarrassing and humiliating.

This is from an organization, a government agency that has caused children under their care to end up dead by actual dangerous people in their care.

I could go on, but anyway, I did the classes and got through the six months.

The case was over not long after so was the nightmare.

In United States, 15.5 million children live in families in which partner violence occurred at least once in the past year, and seven million children live in families in which severe partner violence occurred.

If you don't like the road you're
walking, start paving another one.
—Dolly Parton

CHAPTER 8

Finally

Well, I know as you were reading, thinking over and over again when is she leaving this jerk. Well, the time finally came.

We lost the house. We could have kept it if we could have gotten a lawyer, but with no money and no fight left in me, after three years, it was gone.

Like I said before, God does things for a reason. This was the time for me to go. Alan was going out of town, which he did in the summer for a month for work. There was nothing now tying us together—the kids were older, the house was gone, the perfect time for me to leave while he was away. I didn't let him know anything until he was out of town. Before he left, we had to be out of the house. We decided I would look for a place for us to stay while he was gone. We would stay at my daughter's and my mom and dad's until he came back. When he came back, I told him I wasn't going back, and I had filed for divorce—that was really hard because I knew he was still doing drugs and drinking, needless to say, he did not take it well.

All my fears came true. He came over to my daughter's at night, waited for me when I went to work, harassed me at my parents', left me messages, and called in the middle of the night, threatening to come over. This is the time I was really scared and why a lot of women don't leave. He could have come to my work, killed me then him or someone else. I didn't want anyone getting hurt. He was very unpredictable. When he was on drugs, he told me many times that he would do that very thing if I left him.

They tell you in the victim class if you get a restraining order, that if you think it will make it worse, you might want to think twice about it, after all, it is only a piece of paper. What are they going to do after he kills you and himself? Anyway, finally after the divorce, things did quiet down. He still would leave me messages every now and then, and I still see him around. He still lives in the same town and sees the kids.

It took a long time of looking over my shoulder and being afraid, but after a couple of years, it is less, not gone away completely but less.

Stalking is often an indicator of other forms of violence. Eighty-one percent of women who were stalked by a current or former husband or cohabitating partner were also physically assaulted by that partner. Thirty-one percent of women were sexually assaulted. Abusers use stalking to intimidate and control their victims.

Seventy-six percent of women murdered by an intimate partner were stalked first. Eighty-five of women who survived murder attempts were stalked.

FORGIVENESS

Well, the bruises have all gone away, but the scars will last a lifetime for myself and my kids.

For me, there are some physical scars, but for the most part, there is a permanent scar on my heart and soul. I hope it heals one day, but right now, it's still too fresh. As for my kids, they lost their innocence, their childhood, good times they should have had.

A father that should have put their needs before his own and to be a role model to teach them morals.

To be like a father, should be to their daughters, they should have been daddy's girls treated like princess; they never had that.

I feel so much guilt for that. I try to compensate and be everything—mother and father—but it's hard, very hard, but I try one day, they will all have families of their own, and maybe the bad memories will fade over time and we will make new good memories. I hope so, and I will be there to guide them along the way and hopefully their father will find his way and realize what he's done and be there for them too.

Well, we can dream…

Conclusion

As I was driving to work one day, I heard a song on the radio that reminded me of Al. The words really struck me; he had taken so much from me—my strength, my willpower, all feelings of worth. He made me doubt myself, made me believe I couldn't make it without him.

But now I have my life back—my family, my friends, and I am stronger than I thought I could ever be.

Alan has no hold on me anymore. I look at him now and think how did I ever let that happen to me. It was like a nightmare that took twenty-eight years to wake up from. I now look at the future with hope and optimism not hopelessness and sadness. I know I will meet someone who will love me. God is just waiting for the right time.

Right now, I need to heal. It takes time to recover. Your heart has to mend. Some people might say, "Where was God when you're getting beat?" I felt that way a lot of times, but you know I am here stronger than ever and so is my faith. There are reasons for everything God does. I am in the process of buying a house, which is scary but exciting. I work two jobs—a full-time and part-time that I like, and I finally feel like my life is only getting better.

Back to the song, I wanted to use the lyrics, but it is really hard getting the rights, so the name of the song is "Praying" by Kesha. Please, if you haven't heard it, look up the lyrics or listen to the song; the words are very powerful.

IN A CHILD'S
POINT OF VIEW

My daughter, Elaina, asked if she
Could put down her feelings from her point
Of view. She wanted to tell how it affected
Her. Maybe other children of domestic violence
Have the same feelings.
So these are her words and feelings:

"I could finally breath knowing I didn't
Have to have all that on my conscience.
Felt so good 'cause I could never talk
About it with my family because it was
Too painful, so even though my mom didn't want
To get help at the time, I decided I would
Get it for her.
I didn't want to see her get hurt or
Anyone else for that matter.
I know I did the right thing. I also
Knew they were gonna be mad at me,
But I didn't care. I wanted my family safe and not in danger all the
        time.
My dad was a bad man, but I loved
Him no matter what, and seeing him that
way hurt me. I always thought how could
you do that to your family—you claim to
to love so much.
As I got older, I started to see what

Was going on. I decided to go to my guidance
Counselor at school; it made me feel so much
Better, just talking about it.
Whenever they started fighting, I would stop and
Go to my friend's house next door. She was like
A sister, and her mom was like a second mom.
We would hang out together and talk one day.
She asked me if I was okay, I told her
No. I was sad. I told her about what's
Going on. We went to her mom. I cried,
And she hugged me. It meant so much to me.
I never told them how much that love and
Support meant to me. I am so grateful for them.
My mom has always been there for me.
I guess could say she's supermom; she
Is the strongest person I know. I didn't want
To disappoint her by telling people whenever
It got bad at night. I would put my headphones
On and listen to music; it helped drown
Out the noise and forget at that moment.
What was going on, my paradise?
Music was always my refuge.
When I talked to my guidance counselor,
Everything started happening Department of Children and Families
Came out for months, she would come and check on
Us to make sure no more violence was happening.
She would take a picture of my brother, and I
And check our rooms.
My mother has put up with so much. I'm
Amazed every day.
I can trust her; she's an amazing listener,
And my best friend. She will fight for her
Kids, and I'm proud to call her my mom.
In all honesty, my mom kicks ass!

This next chapter are just text messages left by Al. I had to show those in the divorce to show how he was threatening me. These are not all of them; there were too many to put in, but these give you an idea of where his head was. This is when he found out I was going to file for a divorce. We were not together.

I was staying with my daughter in her apartment; he would sometimes be waiting for me to come out. I had to be at work at 4:00 a.m. to stock, that's why a lot of the calls are early in the morning. He had been doing drugs and drinking all night when he would make the calls. I was always scared. He was around hiding one time I came out to go to work, and he grabbed me and pushed me against the wall. The kids had to come out and threaten to call the cops. Before he would leave, other times, he would go to my work. One time, he had left slut and whore on my windshields. When I came out from work at 10:00 a.m., I noticed it. He had left it early in the morning and had stayed there where everyone could set. I was so embarrassed.

Text Messages

June 2015

Warning!
These are actual text messages from Al.
They are graphic; read at your own risk.

June 16, 3:47 a.m.
Hope your happy with him I'll be there
In the morning I'm coming I'm gonna getting fuck
You're a lying bitch.

June 24, 4:10 a.m.
Your little fucking bitch your not gonna do
This to me you are not gonna do this to me
You are a lying a bitch you're a fucked up bitch.

June 26, 2:41 a.m.
You fucking bitch

These two are from May:

May 17, 2:46 a.m.
Hey call me when you get up I'm
Sitting outside looking at the dam
Staircase I'm drunk as skunk I'm
Not in my car.

May 17, 3:4 a.m.
I'm still sitting outside here saw if
You come out the apartment door
I'm drunk you pussy ass bitch I'm gonna
Find out who your doing.

Text Messages

July 2015

Warning!
These are actual text messages from AL. They are graphic; read at your own risk.

July 12, 2:15, 1:34 a.m.
I know your not fucking me your fucking this guy that's allright that's ok keep fucking him you little bitch keep on you don't have anything to do with me wait till you see what happens wait fucking lying little bitch suck another man's dick I'm gonna man I'm sitting outside here, I'm gonna take care. Of this motherfucking guy I'm gonna take care of him

Text Messages

August 2015

Warning!
These are real text messages from Al. They are graphic; read at your own risk.

Aug., 2:53 p.m.
Fucking bitch Mr. Security gonna take care of your fucking pussy ass huh mother fucker you gonna cheat on me like that motherfucker I'm gonna take care I'll be up there when you go to work today you better hope that mother fucker ain't there.

Aug. 28, 10:51 p.m.
Hope you and your boyfriend are having a good fucking time you little bitch I'm gonna take care of your ass when you get back your tired of it so am I.
Bullshit man allright you're the one sing not me you little slut.

Aug. 31, 12:52 p.m.

Hey I'm back in Tampa I'm headed over to you from your moms to the apartment I'm gonna take care of who's fucking you man you

Warning! These are real text messages from Al. They are graphic; read at your own risk

Cont. Aug 31, 2015
Think you can get away with this bullshit you lying baby doll. I'm gonna fuck him up

Text Messages

September 2015

Warning!
These are real text messages left by Al! They are graphic so read at your own risk.

Sept. 11, 9:16 p.m.
Get your pussy ass divorce you want my address call oll you know your such a pain my ass fucking want money for Sierra now give me a break I'll be home this weekend By Sunday or Monday I'll take are of you and Sierra Hasta Lavista Bitch.

Sept. 6, 9:39 p.m.
That's fucked up going on a date tonight yea I know go ahead do what you got to do ok get your divorce Tuesday I'll be seeing you.

Sept. 30, 2:49 a.m.
Guess you went back to Spanish mother fucker huh fucking bitch I'm gonna see you tomorrow I seen your facebook you're a fucking lying bitch you know that fuck you bitch get your divorce I ain't signing shit I'm gonna fuck your ass up you been fucking him for a long time you bitch keep on playing these games.

Sept. 29, 12:38 a.m.
See you in the morning
I'm in town I'll see you in the morning
your fucked up in the head.

Sept. 30, 3:07 a.m.
I ain't giving you shit I am pissed off.
I'm pissed you know what I've been drinking a little bit what's my fucking Daughter doing up at 3:00

Sept. 30, 2:56 a.m.
How long you been loving that nigger
Mother fucker what is he a nigger or Spanish I'm sorry is he African
American mother fucker.

Text Messages

October 2015

These are real text messages left by AL.
They are graphic so read at your own risk.

October 18, 12:07 a.m.
He's such a fucking man he's taking
Care of your emotional fucking feelings why
Don't you tell the cracker mother fucker.

I am crazy Penny you fucked me over
You fucking to my kids and family away
From me

Sombody's gonna pay for what you did to me

Oct. 17, 11:41 p.m.
Hey you little slut i guess you got your divorce on our anniversary
    you bitch.
I'm in town I'm gonna be over there watching and waiting at your
work whatever I'm gonna do what I gotta do.

Oct. 17, 11:27 p.m.
I was in town looking for your girl
I'm gonna go outer to Chloes to see
What's going on over there hope your around
Man if not I'll be waiting at your work
In the morning for you I want to meet your
New boyfriend bitch your getting your divorce
Because of him I just want to meet him
Me and my boy riding around here we're going
To ride over to Chloe's to see what's up there…
Just want to get with you see what's going

On I'll see you in the morning Happy Anniversary
You slut that's a big step for you bitch all right bye.

Oct. 14, 6:11 p.m.

Hey tell Ivan I know where he lives everything
I'm gonna take care of him when I get
Back you and Ivan have a good time little girl.
Allright bye.

Oct. 14, 6:03 p.m.
You two have your fun while you can ok
I'm going to Hrs and reporting you and
Your little boyfriend.

Oct. 08 2015, 9:56 p.m.

Hey when you motherfuckers getting married
You bitch huh fucking assholes I'm gonna take care of this bullshit
you think you can get away with doing all this shit to me and my
kids that's bullshit.

Oct. 22, 5:01 a.m.
You know what you better call the law
I'm gonna be there I'm gonna take care of
You and your little boyfriend you two have done
Me wrong you need to call me whenever
Your at, you're a lying motherfucker cut.
Bitch know wherever your at I'll take care of you.

Black and Blue

It was wrapped in black and blue
like a gift left under the three…
You'd take it out every so often
wave it around and put it away.
Then you would say you were sorry
kissing all the tears away.
Make promises
I knew you would never keep.
I couldn't stay.
I couldn't go.
It was wrapped in black and blue
like the bruises you left on my body.
No one ever saw those
except you and me.
Careful you were
to not touch the face.
Then you would say you were sorry
kissing all the tears away.
Make promises
I knew you would never keep.
I couldn't stay.
I couldn't go.
I gave you everything
and what I didn't
you took.
It was wrapped in black and blue.
I'll always be wrapped…
in black and blue.

—Glass Poet, 2000

Please don't become a statistic like me.
Get help before it is too late.
Go online or call.
In the US, call the National Domestic Violence Hotline at 1-800-799-7233 (safe) or visit the Domestic Violence Resources Directory for local help.
Call 911 for immediate help.

Signs that your abuser is not changing:
— He minimizes the abuse or denies how serious it really was.
— He continues to blame others for his behavior.
— He claims that you are the one who is abusive.

Psychological abuse includes:
— humiliating the victim
— controlling what the victim can or cannot do
— withholding information from the victim
— deliberately doing something to make the victim feel diminished or embarrassed
— isolating the victim from friends and/or family
— denying the victim access to money or other basic resources
— stalking
— demeaning the victim in public or private
— undermining the victim's confidence and/or sense of self-worth
— convincing the victim she is crazy

Sources
National Coalition Against Domestic Violence
Help Guide.org

ABOUT THE AUTHOR

MSC Photography

Penny Everhart is a Tampa, Florida, native who graduated from Leto High School. Her book *A Family in Fear a Story of Domestic Violence* is her twenty-eight-year account of being a victim. Now she is divorced and out and is a domestic violence survivor. She wants people to understand why men and women stay in the situation, and it's not too late to get out. She hopes to be an inspiration to victims and survivors. You can contact her on Facebook.

CPSIA information can be obtained
at www.ICGtesting.com
Printed in the USA
LVHW111757230821
695908LV00008B/696/J